What Would
1,001 Anytime Questions
It Be
for Anysize Answers
Like...?

D1569073

Chris Cavert & friends

Published by:

Wood & Barnes Publishing
2717 NW 50th
Oklahoma City, OK 73112
(405) 942-6812

Printed in the United States of America
Oklahoma City, Oklahoma
ISBN # 1-885473-33-8

Cover art by Blue Phillips.
Copy editing/design by Ramona Cunningham

To order copies of this book, please call:
Jean Barnes Books
800-678-0621

Acknowledgements

I want to thank all my young friends who contributed to this book. I appreciate the time you gave me and the fun conversations we had along the way.

Allison, Andrew, Barrett, Chris, Clayton, Colleen, Craig, Elizabeth, Hilary, Hunter, James, Jennifer, Jenny, Jonathan, Josh, Kathryn, Katie, Kenny, Lauren, Liz, Mary Carol, Molly, Rachael, Stefanie, Steven, Taylor, Tori, Warren, & Whitney.

A special thanks to my best friend and traveling companion, Susana Acosta. We filled a lot of miles together wondering "what would it be like...?"

Another big thanks goes to Michael and Brian Wood. I sure do appreciate all the great questions. I have enjoyed sharing them with my groups.

To Mom - Your love and spirit get me where I'm going. Thank you so much.

Introduction

What would it be like to have a whole bunch of questions that started with, "What would it be like...?" You're not sure? Well, here is your chance to find out."

These were the first few sentences in the introduction of the "What would it be like..." section in the revised and expanded edition of Games (& other stuff) for Group, Book 1, published in 1999. From this launching pad we have collected over 1000 of these "starters" to help initiate group discussions and conversations. The list that follows can be integrated into group sessions, transition times, etc. Anytime really. I hope you have as much fun with them as we do.

The following questions are presented in closed format. This means they can be answered with one word (usually a feeling word in this case). It is your choice as a facilitator to expand on the questions if you think the individual/group is ready to do so and you have the time. Sometimes it is better to let one-word answers be enough. This can build trust for future discussions.

If you would like to expand on the questions, here's the idea: "What would it be like to move to a new state?" Answers could vary from "scary" to "great, it would get me out of here!" Expanding on the responses is also wide open. "What sorts of things would be scary?" "Why do you want to get out of here?" Then expand upon those answers. You get the idea.

I have presented these questions a couple of ways. I've just opened the book and randomly asked questions. This makes the atmosphere relaxed and non-threatening. Other times I planned ahead and picked questions that related to a certain group discussion that I wanted to have. Both ways have worked well.

Be careful not to spend too much time with one person. I always allow the option to pass or choose a new question. (I usually don't allow more than one chance to pick another question - time problems). If the question seems to cause reactions with others, open the question up to the group. (I usually set up guidelines to prevent others from answering someone else's question or blurting out an answer.) Use your time evenly among the group members to keep the interest going.

Don't forget to take a turn yourself. It is a good way to become part of the group. Have fun with the questions so you'll leave them wanting more!

Chris Cavert

What would it be like...1

- to be respected?
- to ride in an open-air biplane?
- if everyone you knew had a surprise birthday party for you?
- to always be last?
- to catch a fish with your bare hands?
- to conduct an orchestra?
- to wear pajamas all day?
- to read minds?
- to be caught shoplifting?
- if part of your family lived in another country?
- to go on a walk with a two-year-old?
- if you couldn't feel anything?
- to be at the bottom of the food chain?
- to find the city of Atlantis?
- to attend church every day?
- if there came a time when the American Melting Pot were "done"?
- to live on a house boat?
- to catch the bouquet?
- if the world was black and white?
- to liberate a suppressed people?
- to be known as a tattletale?
- to own McDonalds®?
- to get a tattoo?

What would it be like...?.?..?.?.?

- if your signature was worth money?
- to design your own amusement park?
- if there was no competition?
- to be an angel?
- to have anything in the world for one day?
- to get fired from a job?
- to be upside down in a yellow submarine?
- if everyone but you disappeared?
- to work in a greenhouse?
- to be bitten by an animal?
- to be the director of a movie?
- to spill a tray of food in front of a large crowd?
- to have a lifetime subscription to your favorite magazine?
- to wear shorts all the time?
- to communicate with your eyelids?
- to be adopted by a family of a different race than you?
- if you could feel another person's pain?
- to eat a cactus?
- to be snubbed?
- to live on Mars?
- to get at least one hug a day?
- to wash your car in the rain?
- to have your own apartment?
- to be the tallest person in the world?

What would it be like...3

- to be the author of a book on the New York Times® best seller list?
- to build a car from scratch?
- to never take a test?
- to get stuck in the middle of a water slide?
- to have amnesia?
- to meet an alien?
- to have to attend to the king/queen everyday?
- to get up every morning for work at 5:00 a.m.?
- to be the man in the moon?
- to ski on an expert slope?
- to be a street-corner hot dog vendor?
- to grow up with wolves?
- to work on a cattle ranch?
- to walk on crutches for two weeks?
- to add any one thing to your surroundings?
- to knit your own sweater?
- to communicate without words?
- to be divorced?
- if you didn't have to eat?
- to walk across America?
- to live your life in an elevator?
- to never get a hug from anyone?
- to live in a mountain cabin in the winter?
- to own a beach-front condo?

What would it be like...?

- to be the shortest person in the world?
- if you were a teen idol?
- to discover a lost city?
- if there were no more tests?
- to lose your swimsuit in the middle of a water slide?
- to be colorblind?
- to discover a bomb?
- if Scotty beamed you up?
- to go bankrupt?
- to live inside a computer chip?
- to discover a famous shipwreck?
- to be a Pharaoh?
- if your best friend was an animal?
- to be a professional perfume tester?
- to get Gatorade® dumped all over you?
- to stand in a line for 45 minutes?
- to trade places with your parents?
- to eat sushi?
- to go to heaven?
- to live in the dark?
- to be buried in the sand up to your neck?
- to be an inch tall?
- to be Bill Gates?
- to build your own boat?
- to go through school without paper of any kind?

What would it be like...5

- to walk on a tight wire 50 feet above the ground?
- to press a button that launched an atomic bomb?
- to be alive inside another person?
- to do all the work but not get any of the credit?
- to walk the decks of the Nina, Pinta and the Santa Maria?
- to be the blindfold on the Scales of Justice statue?
- to shoot an animal?
- to be a wardrobe consultant?
- to be a miner?
- to watch a baby being born?
- to design your own neon light?
- to always wear a hat?
- if computers never existed?
- to trade places with your brother/sister?
- to never be embarrassed?
- to eat with chopsticks?
- to go rock climbing?
- to live in poverty?
- if you could never hug anyone?
- to be able to walk on water?
- to have your own charge card?
- if you had hair nine feet long?
- to be Bill Gates's child?
- to save the world?

- to earn a varsity letter?
- to body surf waves over eight feet tall?
- to be God?
- to dissect a human body?
- to choose between curtain #1 and $1,000?
- to earn $100,000 a year?
- to be in constant pain?
- if dreams were gateways to the spirits of past relatives?
- to soar like an owl?
- to have a job repairing highways?
- to witness a crime?
- to create a masterpiece?
- to have parents of different races?
- to hike down into a dormant volcano?
- to live the total opposite life you are living now?
- if someone said you were beautiful/handsome?
- to be featured on 60 Minutes®?
- to discover a cure for AIDS?
- to camp out in the snow?
- to rescue someone from a fire?
- if you knew you were going to die today?
- to see what a postage stamp sees?
- to be a doctor who loses a patient?
- if looks were all that mattered?
- to stick your head in the mouth of a lion?

What would it be like...7

- to be a lifeguard?
- to be a master chess player?
- to be a pallbearer in a funeral?
- to help deliver a baby in a taxi?
- if the only clothes you had were hand-me-downs?
- if there were no written communication?
- if you could choose who you wanted to be in your family?
- to feel no happiness?
- to have 10 large marshmallows in your mouth all at once?
- to be lost?
- to live in the White House?
- to get married in a hot air balloon?
- to go skinny dipping?
- to own a solar-powered car?
- to wear braces on your teeth?
- to get the red carpet treatment?
- to write an autobiography?
- to never have to study and get all A's?
- to go cliff diving?
- to be a senior citizen?
- to make your own laws?
- if you could see in the dark without special equipment?

- to be on the barter system?
- to devote your life to the poor and sick?
- to go beyond time and space?
- to be a hydrogen atom?
- to save a baby bird that had fallen from its nest?
- to be a famous dog trainer?
- to work in an animal shelter?
- to do community service?
- to spend a weekend in a penthouse suite?
- to have an identical twin?
- to walk across Africa?
- to live in a world without money?
- to get married in Las Vegas?
- to wear dentures?
- to be Miss Universe/Mr. Universe?
- to appear in a commercial?
- to go ballroom dancing?
- if there were no laws?
- to spend the night in a haunted house?
- to cross a picket line?
- to live in a stress free world?
- to encounter a bear in the wilderness?
- to be a lion tamer?
- to clean other people's houses for a living?
- to be drafted?
- to leave your body to science?

- to fall in the mud with your clothes on?
- if the only way we could communicate was through headphones?
- if there were no families?
- to feel no guilt?
- to eat a worm?
- to lose your way?
- to live off the land?
- to be kissed by a monkey?
- to climb a 70 foot tree?
- to own a jet ski?
- to change one of your facial features?
- if someone asked you for your autograph?
- to create your own candy bar?
- if you could take any subjects you wanted in school?
- to ride in a glider?
- to be liquid?
- to find a winning lottery ticket with someone else's name on it?
- to be the only survivor of a plane crash?
- to be walking in a picket line?
- to be a throw away?
- if parents relied on teachers and legislators to instill morals in their children?
- to be a sequoia tree?

What would it be like...? ? ? ? ? ? ?

- to milk a cow?
- to be a bullfighter?
- to be a school bus driver?
- to be stuck in an elevator for 24 hours?
- to have to choose a new first name on your 21st birthday?
- to be a member of the perfect family?
- to hike for a week in Antarctica?
- to live on your own island?
- if your hair turned gray overnight?
- to have a building named after you?
- to invent a game?
- to be a Buddhist monk?
- to change any one rule?
- to be on a sinking ship?
- to be a professional dog walker?
- to fire a machine gun?
- to work in an assisted-living center?
- to go to a space camp?
- to walk across Russia?
- if you were raised in a commune setting (not knowing parents)?
- to be mistaken for a celebrity?
- if you discovered a genie in a bottle?
- to drive in a monster truck rally?
- to make the trek to Mecca?

What would it be like...11

- •to spend a week with...?
- •if you could contact one person after you died?
- •to be threatened by a bully?
- •if your fantasy became a reality and turned into a nightmare?
- •to be an adult?
- •to dissect a frog?
- •to be a bodyguard to the president?
- •to choose any job you wanted?
- •to help with Habitat for Humanity®?
- •to have a bodyguard?
- •if you didn't own shoes?
- •if you couldn't communicate with others for a week?
- •to pay back all the money your parents ever spent on you?
- •to feel no pain?
- •to drink sour milk?
- •to attend a computer camp?
- •to live in a penthouse?
- •to get stood up by a date?
- •to fall out of a tree?
- •to own your own restaurant?
- •if you couldn't smell?
- •to be the main headline of tomorrow's USA To-day®?

- to make a movie of your life?
- if you got held back a year in school?
- to visit with your favorite sports star?
- to be a genius?
- if you didn't make mistakes?
- if there were no laws?
- if you had to ride a subway to and from work everyday?
- to swim on the back of a whale?
- to play a hammered dulcimer in the forest by a stream?
- if all you had ever known was the family farm?
- to get on your soapbox with a microphone on Pennsylvania Avenue in front of the White House?
- to be a member of the news media?
- to be a diamond cutter?
- to rent out a movie theatre for one night?
- to have no hope?
- to be the only one home watching a scary movie?
- to dress up as Santa Claus?
- if you couldn't listen to music for a year?
- to pay rent to your parents?
- to be the underdog?
- to eat every meal with your hands?

What would it be like...13

- to spend a day in the city of your choice?
- to live in a trash can?
- to be asked out on a date?
- to be caught in a tornado?
- to own a television station?
- to be taller?
- to have a statue made of you?
- to win an Oscar®?
- to be in a school without desks?
- to hold a black belt in a martial art?
- to go fly a kite?
- to be a friend of Robin Hood?
- to not touch or be touched by another living thing?
- not to have any form of government?
- to avoid working because there are better things to do?
- to be a satellite?
- to have to depend on medication to stay alive?
- if a president was impeached by a vote of the people?
- if Jesus had never been born?
- if we didn't use animals as a food source?
- to be a cobbler?
- to be a radio talk-show host?
- to visit a morgue?

- to stay overnight in an airport?
- to wear a tie everyday?
- without music?
- if people never moved away from their families?
- to feel proud of yourself?
- to be without ketchup?
- to journey to the center of the earth?
- to walk across India?
- to live in your car?
- to ask someone out on a date?
- to see a live active volcano?
- to ride into the sunset?
- to own ten acres of land?
- to have no thumbs?
- if someone wrote a song about you?
- to discover a new planet with other living beings?
- to miss your high school graduation?
- if all electronic games were banned?
- to be a plant and always stay in one place?
- if you never needed any sleep?
- to have a clone of yourself?
- to have your name on an office door?
- to try to sell air conditioning to people in an arctic climate?

- to clean up your act?
- if we had the scientific capabilities of creating an immortal human being with perfect characteristics?
- to be put into a zoo?
- to be an Olympic gymnast?
- to be an umpire?
- to pose nude for an art class?
- to experience weightlessness?
- to stay overnight on the street?
- if no one wore shoes?
- to talk with your hands?
- to have a parent in prison?
- to be sad all the time?
- if there were no pizza?
- to go to the Hawaiian Islands?
- to grow up on an army base?
- to go on a blind date?
- to be snowbound in a tent?
- to have your own car?
- to be able to breath underwater unaided?
- to be a superhero?
- to set a world record?
- to go back to school at 40?
- to dribble a basketball across America?
- to be Santa Claus?

What would it be like...?...?...?...?

- to walk through walls?
- to frolic?
- if we all had the same color of skin, hair and eyes?
- to work in customer service for a large department store?
- to be an escape artist?
- to live on the bottom of the ocean in a glass bubble?
- to catch somebody in the act?
- to live by candlelight for a week?
- to spend one day as an animal?
- to be a weather person (meteorologist)?
- if you informed the police of a friend's crime?
- to live to be 100?
- if there were no such thing as underwear?
- if you couldn't read?
- if one of your parents was a police officer?
- to have a fear of crowds?
- to become allergic to your favorite food?
- to ride a motorcycle across the United States?
- if you were chosen to live in a biosphere for one year?
- if you kissed someone and she/he turned into a frog?
- to get caught out in a thunderstorm?

What would it be like...17

- to have your own home?
- to be extremely underweight?
- to be the vice president?
- to sing the "Star Spangled Banner" before a sports event?
- to teach a class of your peers something your good at?
- without sports?
- to be a character in a book?
- to awaken from a coma after five years?
- to have one magical power?
- to sell door-to-door?
- to be a storyteller?
- to live with someone you were afraid of?
- if all women stayed home to raise their children while all men worked outside of the home?
- to be a hamster?
- to be a famous chef?
- to call any one person on the phone and talk for one hour?
- if the drinking age changed to 25?
- to wear the same clothes everyday?
- without books?
- to never have to do chores at home?
- to have a fear of heights?

- to get a pie in the face?
- to travel around the country in a mobile home?
- to live in a castle?
- to kiss your favorite movie star?
- to experience an earthquake?
- to have your own horse?
- if you couldn't hear?
- to be a guest on your favorite television show?
- to invent a new form of transportation?
- to work all day and go to night school?
- if all sports were coed?
- to be immortal?
- to switch places with someone?
- if the world ran out of gas?
- if we were required to go into the same line of work as our father/mother?
- to be a white buffalo?
- to live by faith?
- to care for a baby?
- if animals made no sound?
- to be a master violinist?
- to run out of ideas?
- to receive a large package in the mail?
- to give blood?
- to wear a uniform everyday?

- if we could communicate only through song?
- to have triplets born into your family today?
- to have a fear of the dark?
- to eat a sugarless diet?
- to go to military school?
- to live in nursing home?
- if you had to greet everyone with a kiss?
- to reach the top of the highest mountain?
- to own a sports team?
- if you couldn't see?
- to be a favorite?
- to win a trophy?
- if there were no school?
- to parachute out of a plane?
- to be a friend?
- if everyone in the world were female?
- to be granted just one wish (no wishing for more wishes)?
- if there was no minimum wage?
- to live in a glass house?
- to get your act together?
- to hear voices in your mind?
- to rescue a cat from a tree?
- to be a baby sitter?
- to be robbed?

What would it be like...?...?...?...?

- to tell people your story?
- if every time you went to sleep you had a scary dream?
- if we had to wear family uniforms at all times?
- to be fluent in all languages?
- to be in a family with ten children?
- to share something you are proud of?
- to eat at a restaurant for every meal?
- to travel in a submarine?
- to move in with your grandparents?
- to be in love?
- to be lost in the wilderness?
- to be owned by another human being?
- if you lost your voice completely?
- to be the best?
- to build your own robot?
- to attend school in a one room schoolhouse?
- to go SCUBA diving?
- to be free?
- to be shot from a cannon?
- to be confined indoors for six months?
- if you could have any job you wanted?
- to be a blankie (someone's beloved blanket)?
- to be able to have instant replay anytime, anyplace?
- to be sentenced to death?
- to swim with a dolphin?

- to work in a restroom?
- if your best friend told one of your secrets?
- to give away everything you owned?
- to design your own clothing?
- if you couldn't speak?
- to find out that Darth Vader is your father?
- to get rid of your biggest fear?
- to have your cake and eat it too?
- to go on a jungle safari?
- if you were stranded on an island by yourself?
- to live like the Jetsons®?
- to be loved unconditionally?
- to lose all that you own in a tornado?
- to own a club?
- if your belly button was your mouth?
- if everyone knew who you were?
- if you discovered a cure for the common cold?
- if you weren't allowed to go to school?
- to be a cheerleader?
- to be invisible?
- to do anything you wanted one day, and the next day nobody would remember but you?
- to be without gravity?
- to have your own business cards?
- to travel on a river boat down the Nile?

What would it be like...?

- without kindness?
- to be a kamikaze pilot?
- to be a bird?
- to be a train conductor?
- to lose your wallet?
- if you could join and be accepted by any group?
- if you had to wear a space suit everyday?
- to have your own website?
- to do everything with your family?
- if you couldn't stop laughing?
- to pack your own lunch everyday?
- to have an all-expense-paid, month-long trip?
- if you had to move every two years?
- to be loved by everyone?
- to jump into open ice water?
- to own your own business?
- to have no arms or legs?
- to have famous parents?
- if you won $10,000 but had to give it away?
- to be the principal of a large inner-city school?
- to make the winning shot in a basketball game?
- without electricity?
- to be stranded at sea in a life raft?
- to make your dreams real?

- if it were decided at birth how you would make your living?
- to be a flight attendant?
- to be in orbit?
- to float through the blood stream?
- to be a mountain lion?
- to be a famous artist?
- to have a best friend?
- to do one thing you are not allowed to do?
- if you had to wear a gas mask every time you went outside?
- to have your own mobile phone?
- to be the perfect daughter/son?
- if everyone was afraid of you?
- without snack food at the movies?
- to travel in a yacht?
- to live in a teepee?
- to get stood up at your wedding?
- without flowers?
- to have cosmetic surgery?
- to be a newspaper columnist for a big city newspaper?
- to give away a billion dollars?
- to go to boarding school?
- to miss the winning shot in a basketball game?

24

What would it be like... ? ... ? ... ? ... ?

- to take back one bad thing you did?
- to find a buried treasure?
- to be Batman®?
- to be given a puppy?
- to be a secret agent?

- to propose a toast to your best friend in front of a room full of people?
- to own a motorcycle?
- to have to wear formal clothing all the time?
- to be without a telephone?
- if children were taken from their parents at birth and raised in group homes?
- if vegetables were our only food source?
- to have someone play a practical joke on you?
- to go to a nude beach?
- if you had to live in a giant plastic bubble?
- if someone proposed to you?
- if money grew on trees?
- if everyone looked alike?
- to be a movie critic?
- to know everyone in the whole world?
- if you could trade places with your teacher?
- to ride in a bobsled?
- to have been a member of the Lewis & Clark Expedition?
- to attend a summer sports camp?

- to be charged for a crime you didn't commit?
- to relive one day of your life?
- to be my friend?
- to be a fish?
- to be a baggage handler at an airport?
- to be a pro tennis player?
- to build your own parade float for Macy's Thanksgiving Day Parade?
- to go through a car wash with the top down?
- to find out your best friend had a terminal illness?
- to be raised in an orphanage and never be adopted?
- if insects were our only source of food?
- to be sent to camp every summer for the entire summer?
- to live in a tree house?
- to receive a dozen roses from a secret admirer?
- if the sun were blue?
- to have wings?
- if you were spoken to by God?
- if you were president for one day?
- to be a teacher's favorite student?
- to ride over a waterfall in a kayak?
- to have cars with wings?
- to trade lives with someone else?
- to be my parent?

- if you had to give half of everything you earned to the government?
- to be a dog?
- to work in a cookie store?
- to wake up everyday in the afternoon?
- to find out you had a terminal illness?
- to be in a foster family?
- to eat the same food everyday?
- to go on a picnic every Friday?
- to build your own tree house?
- to have a new last name?
- if the weather was always 72° and sunny?
- to be strong?
- if you were mistaken for a goddess/god?
- to win the lottery?
- to wear a uniform to school?
- to go snowmobiling?
- if drugs were legal?
- to have the ability to see into the future?
- if time stopped?
- to skin a deer?
- to work in a nursing home?
- to read the newspaper everyday?
- to say something nice about yourself?
- to live with a different family?
- to be a camera man for action news?

- to grow and prepare all of your own food?
- to go on a cattle drive?
- to live on the Starship Enterprise®?
- to know who you were going to marry from the time you were born?
- if grass were red?
- to be physically handicapped?
- to be on a game show?
- if you could bring one person back to life?
- to cheat on a test?
- to jump off a cliff?
- to be in a world without deodorant?
- to meet someone just like you?
- if there were no such thing as memory?
- to wake up and be an adult/child?
- to be tickled pink?
- to be my teacher?
- to find a stray dog?
- to work on a cruise ship?
- if things were different?
- to meditate for an hour everyday?
- to build a house with no power tools?
- if your parents broke a promise?
- to drive a car in a demolition derby?
- if you could only eat once a day?

What would it be like...?...?...?...?...?...?

- •to be lost in a foreign country?
- •if everyone lived in apartments?
- •to get a "love" note?
- •if wood didn't burn?
- •to be mentally handicapped?
- •to be born a boy but raised as a girl?
- •to create and run your own museum?
- •to go to school all year long?
- •to be the number one skateboarder in the world?
- •to not have a government?
- •if you woke up to find your skin a different color?
- •to be angry all the time?
- •to discover a new species of animal?
- •to be a private detective?
- •to meet someone who has the same name you do?
- •to "wander off the beaten path"?
- •to stay out as long as you wanted?
- •to be a taste tester for the Jelly Belly Bean® Company?
- •to have a new sister?
- •if you couldn't taste anything?
- •to go on a mission trip outside of the United States?

•to be a medical doctor?

•if you were relocated to a different country with a new identity?

•if someone gave you a wink from across the room?

•without seasons?

•to be beautiful/handsome?

•to be the heroine/hero?

•to be a playwright?

•to be a foreign exchange student?

•to go snowboarding?

•if there were no mirrors?

•to be abducted by aliens?

•to fly on a magic carpet?

•to be a refugee?

•to own a music/video game store?

•to shoot an animal?

•to be a radio DJ?

•to be a scapegoat?

•if we only had cold water showers?

•to have a secret hideout?

•to be a lawyer?

•to have a child?

•to not eat for a week?

•to fly to the moon?

•to work on a farm?

- if you didn't leave your house for a year?
- if you couldn't get married without your family's approval?
- if our only source of water were rain?
- if you couldn't walk?
- to be famous?
- to design your own billboard?
- to go to military school?
- to be voted the "most valuable player" on a sports team?
- if there were no such thing as underwear?
- if the only mode of transportation were pogo sticks?
- to be the opposite gender?
- to know that someone trusted you?
- if you could communicate with animals?
- to be a dentist?
- if everything we used was handmade?
- to have an outhouse for your toilet?
- to be all by yourself for a day?
- to work at a library?
- to choose your own chores?
- to be born a girl but raised as a boy?
- to hike for a week in the desert?
- to be a police officer?
- to live in a monastery?

- if there were no such thing as marriage?
- without the sun?
- if you couldn't use your hands?
- to be infamous?
- to host your own talk show?
- to study abroad for a year?
- to be the world's fastest human?
- if everything you touched turned to gold?
- if breaking wind in public was against the law?
- to travel in a time machine?
- to be the heir apparent to 10 million dollars?
- if we didn't have cats?
- to be happy all the time?
- to be an elephant trainer?
- if you had to walk three miles a day for health reasons?
- without glass?
- to be all alone in the world for a day?
- to be in a musical band?
- if you found out today that you were adopted?
- without hate?
- to go dog sledding?
- to clean the windows of a skyscraper?
- to live in an artist colony?
- to marry a prince/princess?

- if it snowed feathers?
- to lose all your hair?
- to be on the cover of Sports Illustrated®?
- to sell your story to a movie maker?
- if only the rich could afford to go to school?
- to go paintballing?
- to ride across the country in a covered wagon?
- to play the bad guy/girl in a movie?
- to be an Ivy League graduate?
- to be a butterfly?
- to bag groceries for a living?
- without covers?
- to start a club?
- to be by yourself at home for a week?
- to be a missionary worker?
- to never have to clean your room?
- if you were unable to taste sweet?
- to go to Disneyland®?
- to be a fire fighter?
- to live in a one room sod house?
- to receive a diamond ring?
- to have bad acne?
- to be on the cover of People Magazine®?
- to decide what was going to be shown on television?
- if you created a new sport?

- if your horoscope were accurate everyday?
- if things always went exactly as planned?
- to take credit for what someone else did?
- to be an ant?
- to be an active member of Green Peace®?
- to move from a third world country to the United States?
- to lie to your best friend?
- to be a model?
- to pick new parents?
- to only be allowed to communicate with people your own age?
- to be a member of a gang?
- to churn butter?
- to travel across Europe on a train?
- to be a butler/maid?
- to live on a different planet?
- to have a secret admirer?
- to be extremely overweight?
- to be a famous magician?
- to solve the unemployment problem?
- to complete a triathlon?
- if every word started with the letter "B"?
- to have a tracking device put under the surface of your skin?

What would it be like...?

- to spend a week with a person who is 100-years-old?
- to be a house cat?
- to be a trash collector?
- to donate an organ that saved a life?
- without television?
- to be a nurse?
- to have rich parents?
- to be served breakfast in bed?
- to sail around the world?
- to be a professional golfer?
- to live in a log cabin?
- to be infatuated?
- if you had no hair?
- to be the ruler of a small country?
- to have your picture on the front of a tabloid?
- to mingle with the people attending a big Hollywood party?
- to win a gold medal in the Olympics?
- if we all had what we needed - no more, no less?
- if you never had to shop again?
- to think like a computer?
- to create your own animal?
- if we slept during the day and were awake at night?

- without cars?
- to work on an oil rig?
- to share your room with another person?
- to be in a pie-eating contest?
- to travel in a blimp?
- to be a chauffeur?
- to live in an underwater city?
- to be obsessed?
- to wake up and be a different race?
- if you were a movie star?
- to have your own fan club?
- if you discovered the cure for cancer?
- to perform on Broadway?
- if you didn't know anything?
- to have the best birthday party in the world?
- to be on probation, with someone following your every move?
- to be a pizza delivery person?
- to change a baby's diapers?
- to ride across Canada on a bicycle?
- to not have a place to live?
- to lose all your teeth?
- to be voted the most attractive person alive?
- to be a famous musician?
- to discover a new land?

- to make your own laws?
- if you knew everything?
- to discover a secret passage?
- to lose your best friend?
- to speak in front of a large group of your peers?
- to be a Catholic nun/priest?
- to have a disabled brother or sister?
- to ride in a hot air balloon?
- to live somewhere that it rained everyday?
- if we ALL had hairy armpits?
- to direct a movie?
- to spend a week with the President of the United States?
- if we ran out of land for cemeteries?
- to lose a winning lottery ticket?
- if we all had to register our fingerprints and pictures with the FBI?
- to stay in jail overnight?
- to work at a fast food restaurant?
- to be an only child?
- to ride in the space shuttle?
- to live in a cave?
- to change one thing about the way you look?
- to have the energy of Tigger?
- to have a street named after you?

- to be dating a movie star?
- to have private use of an amusement park for a day?
- to control the world?
- if the government regulated the First Amendment?
- to find a hundred dollar bill?
- to be a stunt person?
- to move in with your grandparents?
- to sail the seven seas?
- to live in Russia?
- to be in a boxing match?
- to run out of gas on a date?
- to be a taxi driver in a big city?
- to be a substitute teacher?
- to not know your parents?
- to walk across China?
- to be an all-star wrestler?
- to live in a house with no running water?
- if we couldn't sit down?
- to save someone who was drowning?
- if you were irresistible?
- to witness a robbery?
- to lose everything you owned in a fire?
- to be a psychotherapist?
- to get an allowance for everything you did?

- to be stuck in quicksand?
- to win a Nobel Prize?
- to discover a new civilization?
- without the color white?
- if there were no legal drinking age limit?
- to sleep the night in a graveyard by yourself?
- to drive an armored car?
- to live a certain way to be part of the in-crowd?
- to be alive in another person?
- to drive a tank?
- to save someone who was choking?
- if there were only G-rated movies?
- to be a roadie for your favorite band?
- to ride in a rodeo?
- to be a member of a church youth group?
- to lie to your parents?
- to be a sea captain?
- if you had to fight in a war?
- to be a professional body-builder?
- to live in a cartoon?
- if you woke up and everything you knew to this point had only been a dream?
- if you were lost in a cave?
- to make a living as a street musician?
- to live in the mountains?
- to be there for a friend?

- if the wish you made on a penny and threw into a fountain came true?
- to stay in a hospital overnight?
- to work as a computer game-tester?
- to move to a new state?
- to never see the out-of-doors?
- to go back in time?
- to be an ambulance driver?
- to live in a harem?
- to be on vacation everyday?
- to write a book?
- to be an animator?
- to be a member of the Cleaver family?
- if we ran out of space?
- to go bungee jumping?
- to drive a race car?
- to be a minister?
- if we were all normal?
- if you were pulled over by a police officer?
- to mud wrestle?
- without anesthesia?
- to witness a car accident?
- to drive an eighteen-wheeler across the United States?
- to backpack across the Grand Canyon?

What would it be like...?...?...?...?...?...?

- to be a performer in a traveling circus?
- to be a "test tube" baby?
- to forget your wallet on a dinner date?
- to be in a dance troupe that performed around the world?
- to cut off part of your body for unlimited wealth?
- to climb the stairs of the Statue of Liberty?
- to fly a plane?
- to give your life for someone else?
- if someone said you were stupid?
- to have a paper route?
- to have nine lives?
- if you told your best friend's secret to someone else?
- to be on television?
- to get your finger stuck in your nose?
- to be in a parade?
- to work in a toy factory?
- to be able to communicate with your guardian angel?
- to look out over Paris from the Eiffel Tower?
- if everyone you knew forgot your birthday?
- to be the pitcher for a major league baseball team?
- to have a fairy godmother/father?

- to do your own thing?
- if everything in the world were yellow?
- to be the only one home when someone tried to break in?
- to meet a king?
- to teach an adult something you were very good at?
- to be the quarterback on a football team?
- to pre-plan your funeral?
- if there were no secrets?
- if your favorite movie star became your real life friend?
- to work in a factory?
- if no one lied?
- to go ahead into the future?
- to devote your life to a cause?
- to trust yourself?
- to "rock the boat"?
- to have no fear?
- to be old?
- to open a treasure chest?
- to give?
- to escape from the real world?
- to sail away?
- to realize a dream?
- to have fun?

- •to be yourself?
- •to be satisfied?
- •to make a difference?
- •to have to choose between money and love?
- •to have to choose one of your parents to live with?
- •to feel safe?
- •to have enough?
- •to go camping with your friends for a week end?
- •to have to decide your own discipline?
- •to be a minister?
- •to decide what the weather would be like everyday?
- •to give up your favorite bad habit?
- •to find out that your parents had read your diary?
- •to be a photographer for your high school year book?
- •to be a martyr?
- •to be the one who decided whether or not to declare war?
- •to be a potter?
- •to bloom in the spring and die in the fall?
- •to live in a cottage by the sea?
- •to fall asleep every time you sit down?

- to be the last living member of a race of people?
- to own a vineyard?
- to give up?
- to discover gold in the Yukon?
- to be on board the arc with Noah and all the animals?
- to be a mime in Central Park?
- to be a flower child of the 60's?
- to be a mermaid/man?
- to be a single parent?
- if your nose really did grow every time you told a lie?
- to be responsible?
- to believe in magic?
- to stop living by the clock?
- to be unique?
- to never make comparisons?
- to try to tell someone who had never met you who you are?
- to build a sand castle on the beach?
- to stay in bed all day?
- to stop worrying?
- to marry someone like me?
- to be down to your last dollar?
- to face the facts?

- to go to a luau?
- to stutter?
- to be a member of high society?
- to be a clown?
- to belong?
- to write over a thousand "What Would It Be Like...?'s?

?

About the Author

Chris Cavert has been a teacher for over 20 years. He has worked with youth and adult groups of all ages. Chris holds a Physical Education teaching degree from the University of Wisconsin-LaCrosse, and nears completion of a Masters degree in Experiential Education from Mankato State University.

Some of his first writing was published in the best selling *Chicken Soup for the Soul* series by Jack Canfield and Mark Victor Hansen, and his activities have been published in books by Karl Rohnke, Jim Cain and Berry Jolliff. Since then Chris has written:

E.A.G.E.R. Curriculum;
Games (& other stuff) for Group, Books 1 & 2;
Games (& other stuff) for Teachers;
Affordable Portables: A workbook of activities and problem solving elements; and
50 Ways to Use Your Noodle: Loads of land games with foam noodle toys (coauthored with Sam Sikes).